CROSS-SECTIONS
THE M109A6
PALADIN

by Steve Parker
illustrated by Alex Pang

Capstone
press®

Mankato, Minnesota

Edge Books are published by Capstone Press, a Coughlan Publishing Company,
151 Good Counsel Drive, P.O. Box 669, Mankato, Minnesota 56002.
www.capstonepress.com

Library of Congress Cataloging-in-Publication Data
Parker, Steve.
   The M109A6 Paladin/by Steve Parker; illustrated by Alex Pang.
   p. cm.
   Summary: "Provides an in-depth look at the M109A6 Paladin, with detailed
cross-section diagrams, action photos, and fascinating facts"—Provided by publisher.
   Includes bibliographical references and index.
   ISBN-13: 978-1-4296-0094-1 (hardcover)
   ISBN-10: 1-4296-0094-2 (hardcover)
   1. M109 Paladin (Howitzer)—Juvenile literature. I. Title.
UF652.P37 2008
623.4'2—dc22   2007012799

Designed and produced by

David West Children's Books
7 Princeton Court
55 Felsham Road
Putney
London SW15 1AZ

Designer: Rob Shone
Editor: Gail Bushnell

Photo Credits
U.S. Army, 1, 6t, 7b, 18, 21, 22, 24, 28–29, 29; U.S. Air Force, 4–5; Bukvoed, 7t;
Marcel Jussen, 11; Michael G. High, 12, 16; BAE Systems, 14, 28b; U.S. DoD, 20;
Quistnix, 28t; Imperial War Museum, 6b

1 2 3 4 5 6 12 11 10 09 08 07

TABLE OF CONTENTS

M109A6 PALADIN

The U.S. M109 howitzer is the world's most successful large gun-type weapon which is self-propelled (SP). This means it has an engine and does not have to be towed.

The first M109s went into service more than 40 years ago in 1963. They have seen action in many conflicts, from Vietnam to Iraq. They have also been sold to more than 25 other nations.

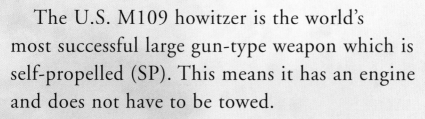

The M109 was gradually improved as the M109A1, M109A2, and so on. In 1993, a hugely improved version of the M109 began service, the M109A6.

The M109A6 is code-named Paladin. This is an ancient Roman word which means a heroic champion who defends a worthy cause. The M109A6 continues that legend.

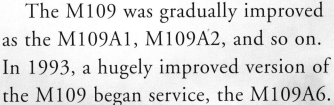

The M109A6 uses its great firepower from slightly farther back in the combat zone. It supports troops and vehicles at the front line.

Howitzer History

The M198 is a towed howitzer that is used by the U.S. military. It has a similar barrel size to the M109.

The Paladin is a type of artillery, or large firing weapon, called a howitzer.

GUNS, HOWITZERS, MORTARS

Most guns tend to fire low and fast. A gun's bullets or shells hit the side of their target. A mortar fires high but not as far. A howitzer is between these two. It has a fairly short, wide barrel. Its shells or other projectiles are powerful, but travel quite high and slowly.

CANNONBALLS TO CHARGES

Howitzers were first used in the 1700s. They were mounted on two-wheeled carriages pulled by horses. At first they fired solid cannonballs. Then they fired hollow iron shells filled with explosives.

The British Gun Carrier Mark 1 was developed from the Mark 1 tank in 1917. It was the first self-propelled howitzer weapon.

The United States made almost 3,500 M7 Priests. They were successful in World War II and also in the Korean War (1950–1953).

The M109A2/A3 went into service in 1980. It had 27 improvements over the M109A1. Its M185 howitzer had a range of about 14 miles (23 kilometers).

WORLD WAR ACTION

During World War I (1914–1918), howitzers rained down massive destruction onto nearby enemy trenches. In World War II (1939–1945), most howitzers were towed, and tanks took over the main action. In the 1950s, the United States started to design a fast, mobile, self-propelled howitzer. This became the M109.

CROSS-SECTION

The Paladin is a totally self-contained fighting machine. It can shoot at nearby enemy positions that its crew can see. Or it can receive orders by radio and fire shells many miles into enemy territory.

The Paladin looks similar to a tank. It has a big gun on a turning turret, a boxlike main body called the hull, and go-anywhere tracks. But it is less heavily armored than a tank because it is less likely to see front-line action. The Paladin's gun is also a howitzer type, with a relatively wide barrel.

ENGINE
See pages 10–11

TRANSMISSION
See pages 10–11

MAIN GUN
See pages 20–21

GUN LOCK
See pages 14–15

M109A6 PALADIN
Length: 32 feet (9.7 meters)
Width: 10 feet (3 meters)
Turret height: 9 feet (2.8 meters)
Weight: 63,270 pounds
     (28,700 kilograms)
Maximum speed: 38 miles
     (61 kilometers) per hour
Range: 186 miles (300 kilometers)

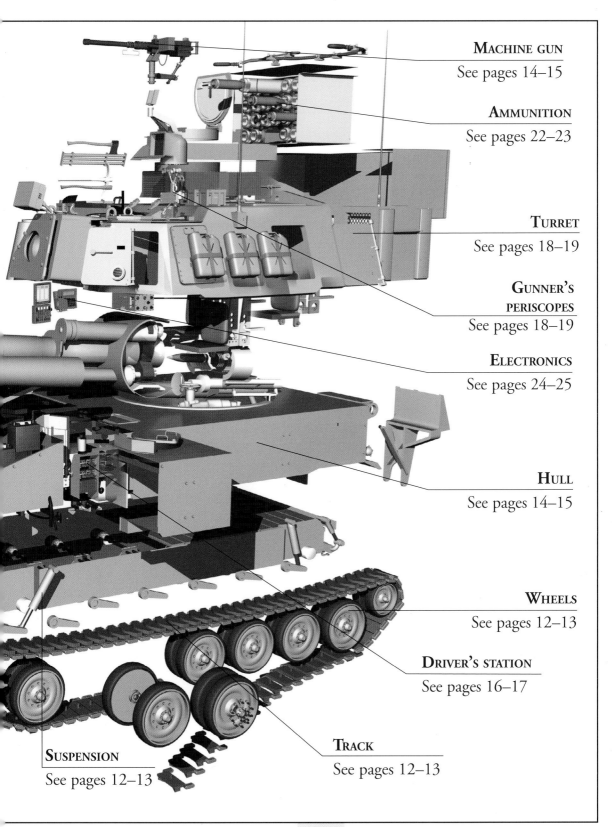

MACHINE GUN
See pages 14–15

AMMUNITION
See pages 22–23

TURRET
See pages 18–19

GUNNER'S PERISCOPES
See pages 18–19

ELECTRONICS
See pages 24–25

HULL
See pages 14–15

WHEELS
See pages 12–13

DRIVER'S STATION
See pages 16–17

SUSPENSION
See pages 12–13

TRACK
See pages 12–13

THE ENGINE

The Paladin's power plant is an 8-cylinder turbocharged diesel engine. It turns the drive wheels for the tracks. It also powers the generator for on-board electricity.

The Detroit Diesel engine is tough, reliable, and easy to repair. It is located inside the front right of the hull. It can be serviced in position, but it is sometimes removed through a hatch for fuller maintenance and repair. The engine powers the Paladin to a top speed of 38 miles (61 kilometers) per hour.

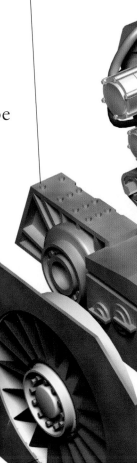

TRANSFER ASSEMBLY

The transfer assembly passes on the turning power of the engine to the transmission.

ENGINE FANS

The fans keep the liquid-cooled engine at the right temperature to work at full power.

ENGINE

The engine block has eight pistons inside cylinders. It has a two-stroke cycle, with fuel exploding for every up-down piston movement.

A Paladin engine is tested in the workshop. It is checked for unusual noises or vibrations which could indicate faults.

EXHAUST

The exhaust is designed to help remove engine heat for cooler, more efficient running. The exhaust gases also recycle their energy by spinning the turbocharger fan. This forces more air and fuel into the cylinders for extra power.

TRANSMISSION

The Allison XTG-411-4 oil-cooled transmission has four forward gears and two reverse gears. The gears alter the speed of the output shafts. These shafts turn the drive wheels attached to the tracks.

Position of engine on the Paladin

ENGINE SPECIFICATIONS
Detroit Diesel type 8V-71T
Capacity: 568 cubic inches (9.3 liters)
Power output: 440 horsepower (hp)

THE WHEELS AND TRACKS

The Paladin is a fully tracked vehicle. It can cross trenches, ride over rocks, and drive over soft mud.

The tracks are like a "rolling road" that continually lays itself under the wheels. The track design means there is a large area in contact with the ground. This spreads the Paladin's weight so it does not get bogged down in sand or mud. However the tracks need lots of energy to move them so the Paladin uses large amounts of fuel.

FINAL DRIVE ASSEMBLY

The final drive assembly transfers the engine's turning power from the transmission and the output shaft to the drive wheel.

The toothed drive wheels (one on each side) are the only wheels powered by the engine.

DRIVE WHEEL

The 10 teeth of the drive wheel fit into slots in the track. They pull the track around and around in a never-ending loop.

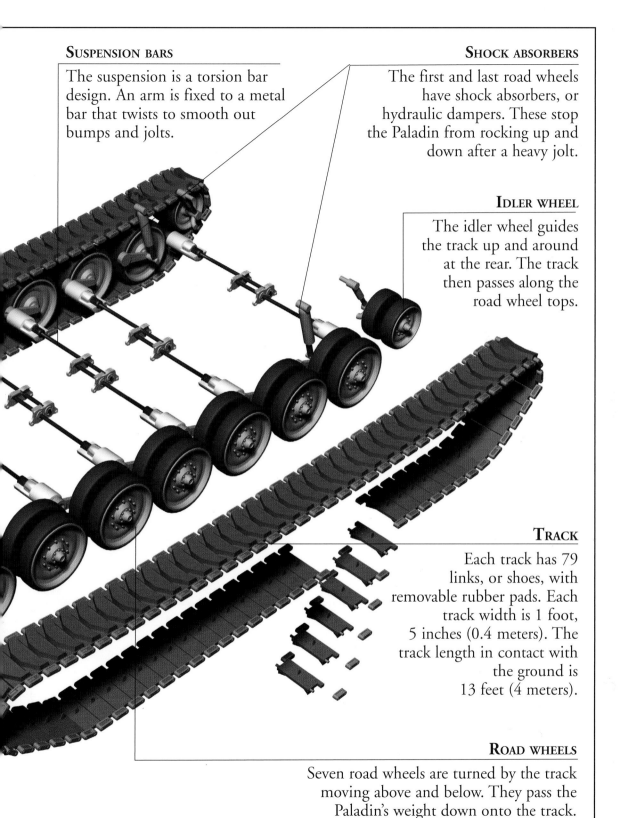

SUSPENSION BARS

The suspension is a torsion bar design. An arm is fixed to a metal bar that twists to smooth out bumps and jolts.

SHOCK ABSORBERS

The first and last road wheels have shock absorbers, or hydraulic dampers. These stop the Paladin from rocking up and down after a heavy jolt.

IDLER WHEEL

The idler wheel guides the track up and around at the rear. The track then passes along the road wheel tops.

TRACK

Each track has 79 links, or shoes, with removable rubber pads. Each track width is 1 foot, 5 inches (0.4 meters). The track length in contact with the ground is 13 feet (4 meters).

ROAD WHEELS

Seven road wheels are turned by the track moving above and below. They pass the Paladin's weight down onto the track.

THE HULL

The main body of the Paladin is known as the hull. It is made from armored metal. Holes, or hatches, let the crew enter and leave. They are closed by armored hatch doors.

This Paladin has its barrel locked and command hatch open, ready to roll.

There are three main compartments inside the Paladin. These are the engine compartment, the driver's compartment, and the turret.

The interior of the Paladin has protective coverings called spall liners. If the Paladin is hit by enemy fire the outside can be damaged. But the spall liners prevent the metal inside from shattering.

GUN LOCK

The gun lock holds the howitzer barrel firmly in place as the Paladin travels.

FORWARD ARMOR

The main walls of the hull are made from strong aluminum alloy. They are 1.25 inches (3.2 centimeters) thick.

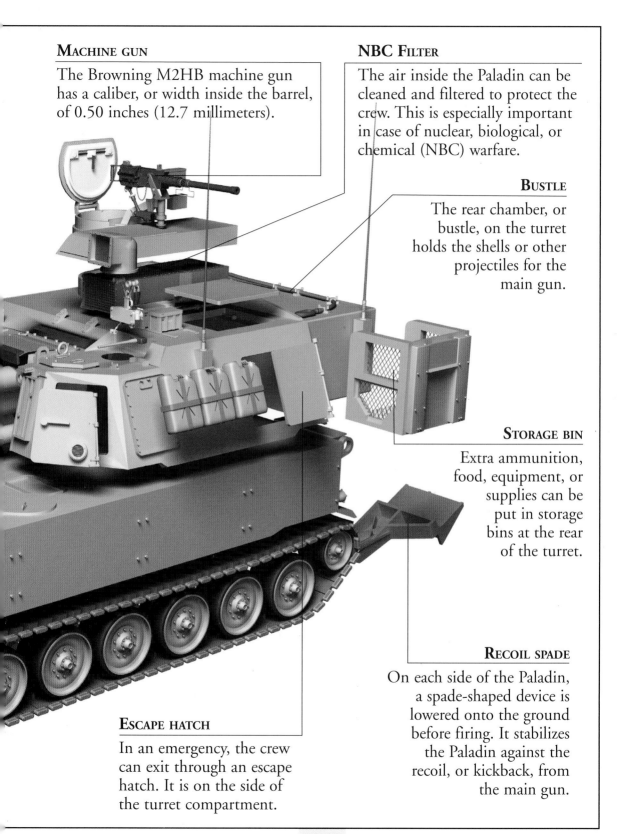

MACHINE GUN

The Browning M2HB machine gun has a caliber, or width inside the barrel, of 0.50 inches (12.7 millimeters).

NBC FILTER

The air inside the Paladin can be cleaned and filtered to protect the crew. This is especially important in case of nuclear, biological, or chemical (NBC) warfare.

BUSTLE

The rear chamber, or bustle, on the turret holds the shells or other projectiles for the main gun.

STORAGE BIN

Extra ammunition, food, equipment, or supplies can be put in storage bins at the rear of the turret.

RECOIL SPADE

On each side of the Paladin, a spade-shaped device is lowered onto the ground before firing. It stabilizes the Paladin against the recoil, or kickback, from the main gun.

ESCAPE HATCH

In an emergency, the crew can exit through an escape hatch. It is on the side of the turret compartment.

THE DRIVER'S STATION

A circular hatch that opens to the left leads down into the driver's compartment. This compartment has its own heater and air purifier.

The driver sits in his own compartment at the left front of the hull. The engine is just to his right.

The driver does not have a window or windshield. This would be too dangerous if the Paladin came under enemy fire. The driver's view is through M45 periscopes. These resemble angled telescopes and reflect the scene outside down into the driver's compartment. On the outside, they can be covered by metal flaps if there is a danger of damage. The driver talks to other crew members through an intercom.

STEERING THE PALADIN

Tracked vehicle wheels do not turn to the side. The steering yoke alters the speed of the drive wheels. This makes the track on one side move faster or slower than the other track. With one track still, and the other moving, the Paladin almost turns on the spot.

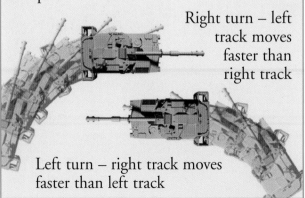

Right turn – left track moves faster than right track

Left turn – right track moves faster than left track

Position of driver on the Paladin

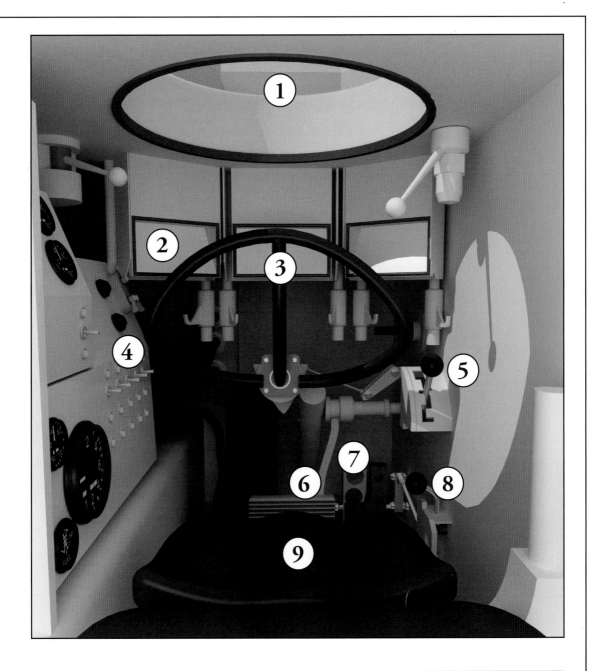

KEY TO COCKPIT CONTROLS
1. Driver's hatch
2. Periscopes
3. Steering yoke
4. Movable control panel
5. Gear shift lever
6. Brake pedal
7. Accelerator
8. Seat raising arm
9. Seat (with back lowered)

THE TURRET

The turret, or fighting compartment, is the control and firing center of the Paladin. Its standard crew of three includes the commander, the gunner, and the cannoneer.

The commander gives orders to the rest of the crew. He also communicates with other Paladins and the command center.

The gunner's main role is to aim the barrel. He makes the turret turn around, or traverse, and the gun barrel rise, or elevate. The cannoneer selects shells or other ammunition and loads and checks the gun before firing.

The commander helps the cannoneer load a shell into the breech of the Paladin's main gun.

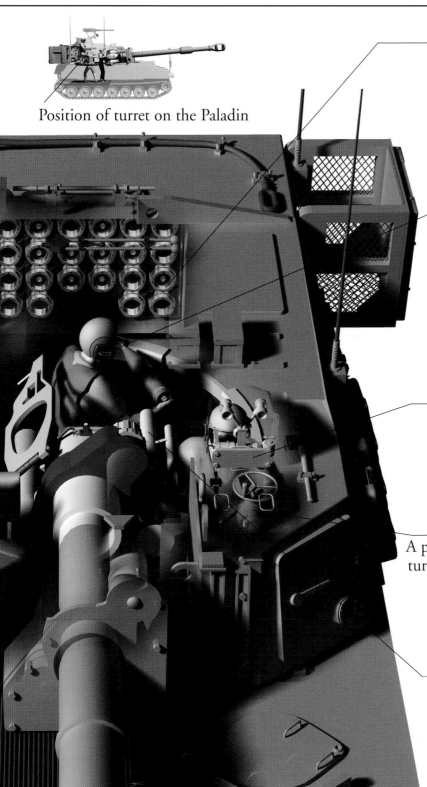

Position of turret on the Paladin

AMMUNITION

The turret bustle stores a basic load of 39 standard 155 mm shells. It can also hold a mix of other projectiles.

INTERCOM SYSTEM

All crew members are linked by the VIC-1 internal communication system, or intercom. They have helmet headphones and face microphones.

GUNNER'S PERISCOPE

The gunner can see nearby targets through the M118C magnifying periscope.

TURRET TRAVERSE MECHANISM

A powerful electric motor turns the turret. It can go around once in 32 seconds.

GUN RAMMER

The powered rammer loads the shells into the breech. It does this even when the barrel is pointing up at a high angle.

THE GUN AND BREECH

The Paladin's main weapon is the M284 howitzer gun. It can be aimed manually by the gunner. The on-board computer also may automatically aim it using radio information from central command.

In the heat of battle, the M284 gun can be reloaded, checked, and fired within 15 seconds.

RECOIL CYLINDER

As the shell blasts out of the barrel, it produces a recoil, or kickback force. This force is absorbed by the recoil cylinder.

BREECH MECHANISM

The shell or other projectile is loaded into the breech. Then the breech chamber is sealed. This means the hot gases from firing the shell do not escape backward. They force the shell forward along the barrel.

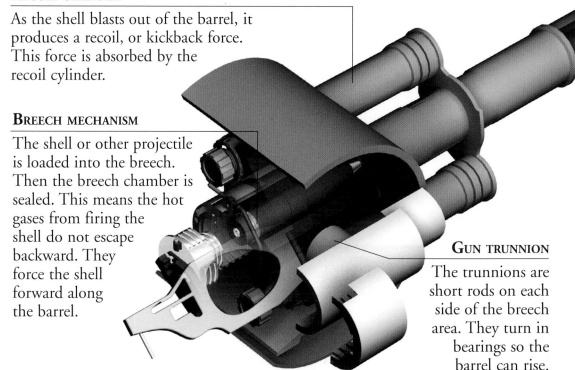

GUN TRUNNION

The trunnions are short rods on each side of the breech area. They turn in bearings so the barrel can rise.

The Paladin can stop, prepare, aim, and fire in less than a minute. Its standard rate of firing is once per minute. But if needed it can fire four times in one minute. All of the actions for firing are carried out inside the Paladin, which greatly increases crew safety.

MUZZLE BRAKE

The muzzle brake slows the shell and redirects some of the gases from the firing. This helps to reduce the recoil.

BORE EVACUATOR

The bore evacuator holds some of the poisonous hot gases as the shell leaves. It then releases them out of the barrel end. This stops them from flowing into the Paladin when the breech is opened.

When the M284 fires, a roar of hot gases blasts the shell along the barrel. The shell speeds out of the barrel's open end, or muzzle. However the heat, noise, and smoke can give away the Paladin's position to the enemy.

AMMUNITION

The Paladin's M284 is 155 mm caliber, meaning the width of the hole inside the barrel is 155 millimeters (6.1 inches). The gun can fire a wide range of 155 mm shells and other ammunition.

A modified version of the M109 is the M992 FAASV, or Field Artillery Ammunition Supply Vehicle. It carries extra shells or other ammunition for Paladins.

In Western nations, 155 mm is a standard gun size. There are many different designs of 155 mm shells and other projectiles. They are fired by an explosive propellant which is part of each round of ammunition.

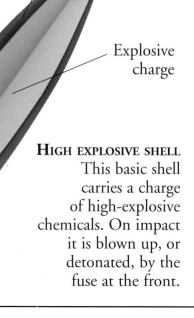

Metal casing

Fuse

Explosive charge

PROPELLANT
The propellant chemical behind the shell is lit, or ignited. This produces an explosion of hot gases that hurls the shell along the barrel.

HIGH EXPLOSIVE SHELL
This basic shell carries a charge of high-explosive chemicals. On impact it is blown up, or detonated, by the fuse at the front.

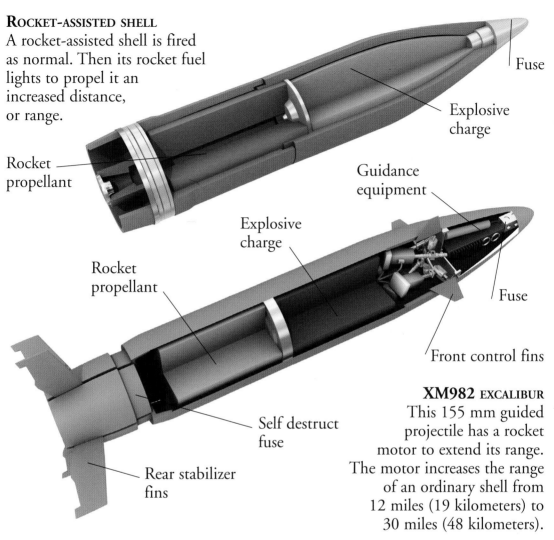

ROCKET-ASSISTED SHELL
A rocket-assisted shell is fired as normal. Then its rocket fuel lights to propel it an increased distance, or range.

Fuse

Explosive charge

Rocket propellant

Guidance equipment

Explosive charge

Rocket propellant

Fuse

Front control fins

Self destruct fuse

Rear stabilizer fins

XM982 EXCALIBUR
This 155 mm guided projectile has a rocket motor to extend its range. The motor increases the range of an ordinary shell from 12 miles (19 kilometers) to 30 miles (48 kilometers).

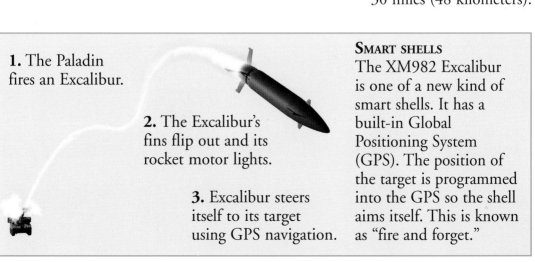

1. The Paladin fires an Excalibur.

2. The Excalibur's fins flip out and its rocket motor lights.

3. Excalibur steers itself to its target using GPS navigation.

SMART SHELLS
The XM982 Excalibur is one of a new kind of smart shells. It has a built-in Global Positioning System (GPS). The position of the target is programmed into the GPS so the shell aims itself. This is known as "fire and forget."

ELECTRONICS

The first M109s were made more than 40 years ago. The modern M109A6 Paladin vehicle is similar to the older M109. But the electronic equipment is very different.

Upgrades have packed the M109A6 Paladin with the latest computers, radios, GPS, and many other electronic systems.

The M992A2 FDCV, or Fire Direction Center Vehicle, has the basic M109 hull, tracks, and engine. But it has no turret. It is modified as a command center for groups of Paladins and other combat vehicles.

The FDCV can be fitted with a tall antenna, or aerial. FDCVs act as mobile command posts to organize the missions.

COMMUNICATION SYSTEM
Information passed by radio includes firing positions and target locations. The signals are digitally coded so they are clear and reliable, but also secret.

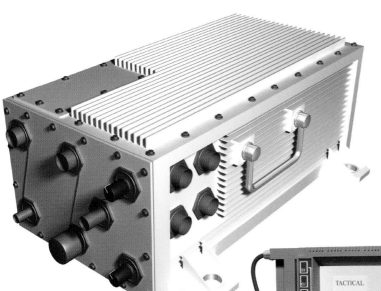

Automatic fire control system

The Automatic Fire Control System, or AFCS, tells the driver where to position the Paladin. It automatically unlocks the gun, turns the turret, and raises the barrel. Then the gunner can check the aim.

Digital data display

The display shows the position of the Paladin on a local map. It also shows the position, direction, and range of the target.

PDIU

PDIU stands for the Prognostic/ Diagnostic Interface Unit. The PDIU shows which parts of the Paladin will wear out or fail soon (prognosis). In a breakdown, it indicates the fault (diagnosis).

THE MISSION

One of the Paladin's main roles is to fire powerful explosives from a relatively long range. It supports troops in the thick of combat. Paladins can also be used to disable enemy guns, tanks, and missiles.

2. Central command radios a group of four Paladins. They head off fast to their firing position.

The Paladin can move into position and prepare to fire very quickly. It then changes back to travel condition and speeds on before the enemy strikes back. This ability to fire and escape is called "shoot and scoot."

1. A scout vehicle detects enemy guns and contacts central command.

3. Less than a minute after the Paladins stop, they fire and hit their target.

4. Enemy radar locks onto the origin of the Paladin's shells. Enemy missiles launch a counter strike.

5. But the Paladins have already moved away. The enemy missiles miss their target. The Paladins move to a new attack position. They fire against the enemy missile launchers.

THE FUTURE

By the mid-2000s, U.S. forces had almost 1,000 M109A6 Paladins. They have been reliable and successful. But other countries are producing more powerful designs of the heavy howitzer.

Realizing this fact, the U.S. also made plans to make better howitzer-type vehicles. The U.S. had planned a new big gun to replace the Paladin. It was called the M2001 Crusader, and it began development in the 1990s. The Crusader would have been faster and more powerful than the Paladin. But in 2002, the U.S. government cancelled the project.

The German-made PzH 2000 is an advanced howitzer designed in the 1990s. It shoots faster and more accurately than the Paladin.

The AS-90 Braveheart, a British self-propelled 155 mm howitzer, went into service in 1993.

The Crusader would have been able to fire just 15 seconds after stopping.

The NLOS-C will need only two crew members to operate it. The firing system of the NLOS-C will be partly operated by a computer.

Eventually the Paladin will be replaced by the more accurate Non Line of Sight Cannon (NLOS-C). The NLOS-C is part of the U.S. military's planned Future Combat Systems, or FCS. The FCS will make use of the most modern military vehicles and equipment. But Paladins are still going to be an important part of the U.S. military until about 2030.

GLOSSARY

armor (AR-mur)—a protective metal covering

exhaust (eg-ZAWST)—very hot gases leaving an engine

horsepower (HORSS-pou-ur)—the measurement of an engine's power, abbreviated as hp

hull (HUL)—the main body or casing of a tank or similar armored vehicle, such as the Paladin

mission (MIH-shuhn)—a task given to a person or group

radar (RAY-dar)—equipment that uses radio waves to find or guide objects

suspension (suss-PEN-shun)—the tilting arms, springs, dampers and other parts that smooth out road bumps so a vehicle's ride is more comfortable

track (TRAK)—on a tank or tracked vehicle, the links that form an endless loop, like a conveyor belt or "rolling road"

transmission (tranz-MISH-uhn)—gears and other parts that transfer the power from the engine to the wheels

READ MORE

Baker, David. *M109 Paladin.* Fighting Forces on Land. Vero Beach, Fla.: Rourke, 2007.

Green, Michael, and Gladys Green. *Self-Propelled Howitzers: The M109A6 Paladins.* War Machines. Mankato, Minn.: Capstone Press, 2005.

Hamilton, John. *Weapons of the 21st Century.* War in Iraq. Edina, Minn.: Abdo, 2004.

INTERNET SITES

FactHound offers a safe, fun way to find Internet sites related to this book. All of the sites on FactHound have been researched by our staff.

Here's how:
1. Visit *www.facthound.com*
2. Choose your grade level.
3. Type in this book ID **1429600942** for age-appropriate sites. You may also browse subjects by clicking on letters, or by clicking on pictures and words.
4. Click on the **Fetch It** button.

FactHound will fetch the best sites for you!

INDEX